C000051731

swiftly

RACHEL MADELINE

SWIFTLY

Copyright © 2021 Rachel Madeline

All rights reserved.

ISBN: 9798517107602

THANK YOU

To my wonderful friends and family: thank you for encouraging me to reach for my dreams even when I thought they were unattainable.

To Taylor: thank you for writing masterpieces that were the basis for this entire book.

To me: this is your first book, I hope you're proud of it.

TAYLOR SWIFT

'PS: To all the boys who thought they would be cool and break my heart, guess what? Here are 11 songs written about you. HA."

Tim McGraw

Summer attached to your skin like honey

sticky sweet with just a hint of salt.

As I sat across from you, eyes glazed,

the air conditioning blowing over the road,

and my feet resting on the tattered dash

you would turn on my favorite song.

When the air thickened into frost

your passenger seat laid vacant,

only strands of my hair left behind.

After three years, I can't help but wonder

when you hear those soft opening chords

do you still see me there next to you?

Picture to Burn

I'd rather set fire to every memory of us

and let the wind carry away the ashes of our history

than watch you write my name down at the very bottom

on your list of the things you love, below your own sad ego.

Teardrops on My Guitar

I always thought losing you would be the hardest burden to bear.

Suddenly one day you wouldn't be there to hear my dumb jokes

that I purposefully made terrible just for your laugh to echo in the hall.

You would keep me up at night, but in a much different way;

In a way I would be mourning the death of everything we had

instead of pacing back & forth asking myself "what if we were more?".

I would spend every moment writing about the way you made me feel

until all my pens ran dry, and tears turned pages into abstract art.

It turns out that I was wrong all along.

The hardest burden was to watch you choose someone else

but keep me as platonically close as you could handle.

And I'm not the cause for your laugh anymore

and you're the lead in of all my nightmares

and the reason my work is undecipherable.

A Place in This World

Each person in the world is a piece

of the greatest puzzle to exist.

No two are exactly the same,

cut from the same basic material

but uniquely curved and etched

to fit into their unique space.

No one else can replace it

or be reshaped to match,

we all have a place reserved for us.

I spend my days praying to know

where my serrated edge lay

in relation to the rest of the picture.

Cold As You

In those long, frigid months

I gave you my large coat,

every beautiful blue sky,

every dream I held dear,

every ounce of my pride,

every damn thing I had.

Stripped of all that's cozy and bright,

reality hit me like a blizzard in January.

I could be on the verge of frostbite

and would still be significantly warmer

than the cockles of your heart.

The Outside

Someone once told me that

all the answers I seek exist

just beyond the entryway.

Rust cautiously hugs the hinges

inviting my touch on the handle

just to spite me with the stick of the lock.

In the biting cold I can't help but wonder:

Will doors ever open for someone

as extraordinarily ordinary as me?

Tied Together With A Smile

Porcelain

silky, cool porcelain against my face.

The edges hug my jaw like lover's hands,

emulating the shape of the shiny smile

permanently painted on the other side.

It has taken a lifetime to craft to its perfection.

This mask is all that is left between pride

and the crushing reality of my own sadness.

Stay Beautiful

That face launched a thousand fictitious stories

authored only by my restless self-conscious.

Each one starts with becoming the person

every set of starstruck eyes said

you would be

and ends with all signs leading to my door.

When Helios's Chariot rises again, I sit and wait

for the hollow knock against chipped blue paint

with you standing there, still beautiful as ever.

Should've Said No

My weakness was always your left dimple

and how it carved a deep well into your cheek

when you flashed a smile reserved for only me.

Yours was a pair of deep green eyes and crimson lips

that made you for a moment forget your own name

and place my existence in a box of things omitted.

Mary's Song

It's when those eyes, that light up the velvet sky,

look in mine that I give in to you.

You can take my heart and lead me anywhere.

To beneath the backyard tree where your laugh

danced a foxtrot with the auburn falling leaves

while you told me about a life far from here.

To the passenger seat of your first car

with your face in the glow of the faded red,

I realized I would only ever love that smile.

To that empty street corner in the rain

shivering as you held me closer than before,

letting our fight wash away with the night.

To the end of an aisle lined with pews

looking at me like there was never another

who could be standing there whispering "I do".

Our Song

The softest wheeze of your breath

against my shoulder in the morning glow.

Your voice dry and hoarse in the air

from hours of easy, light conversation.

Scrapping of keys against the counter

as you're welcomed home with glee.

Shuttering of closing eyelashes

as you pay me a wink across the room.

Compile every ounce of sound

into an audio file only we can hear.

A song made just unique to us.

I'm Only Me When I'm With You

If you took an axe and split me in half

it could be found I'm really two souls:

the one dancing around in daylight

made for the criticizing eyes of others

and one bathed in iridescent nightfall

who awakens only in your presence.

Invisible

For you I'm a shop window:

standing firm against the elements

regardless of how severe they rage.

Yet, completely translucent in your eyes

as your peer right through my being,

eyeing the goods on the other side.

Perfectly Good Heart

No matter how much time has passed I can still remember
your name as I run a finger over the scarred tissue where
stitches once laid. By touch alone, anyone could tell the
patchwork was inconsistent, sloppy even; but then again, what
could anyone expect from my first time sewing my heart back
together

SWIFTLY

FEARLESS

"To me, fearless is not the absence of fear. It's not being completely unafraid. To me, fearless is having fears. Fearless is having doubts. Lots of them. To me, fearless is living in spite of those things that scare you to death."

<u>Fearless</u>

Your voice telling me all the things

that straighten my spine in fear:

We could run to the horizon line,

become anyone we've wanted to be,

see everything we dream about daily.

With my stomach a fisherman's knot

and your warm palm against mine,

I am the bravest I have ever been.

<u>Fifteen</u>

The age you finally are no longer a child, but not quite an adult. You don't know a thing about taxes or the career you will inevitably have, but you understand love, or rather the idea of love that you've created in your head. Too young to know that not everyone who utters three loaded words to you will stay true to them, but too old to not take responsibility for not seeing all the red flags sooner. Emotionally driven and feeling as if the ground below your feet has suddenly vanished, the thought won't even cross your mind that in years to come you will forget what locker yours is, the smell of the classroom you had history in, or the name of the one who broke you first.

Love Story

A vengeful breeze blew the pages wide open

revealing a story of the brushing of hands,

hushed voices down shadow clad hallways,

coded letters stowed away in hidden crevices,

stolen breathless moments beneath moonlit ivy.

Paragraphs and stanzas of star-crossed prose

beginning with the momentary meeting of eyes

and ending with the greatest tale of tragic love

two young, fated souls have ever dared endure.

Hey Stephen

Everyone would risk their humility

to be able to claim your smile

is the work of their actions.

They'd scream "how high?"

if you uttered the word "jump"

and toss pebbles at your window

to re-enact movie designed love.

For you, I would go even further

and risk every gram of my soul

writing this poem for only you.

White Horse

As children, we were plied with fairy tales

stories of balls and yearning damsels

for our unblemished minds to dream of.

So, imagine my disappointment when

I handed you my storybook dreams

filled with landscapes of haunted forests

and crystalline streams home to all

the happy endings I envisioned for us

and you broke them with realistic words

"I can't do this anymore."

You Belong With Me

Our future together comes down

to a single fleeting moment of clarity

you'll feel when you follow

the hand twisted with yours

all the way up the arm to the face,

wishing you saw my blossoming rose cheeks.

Breathe

It's easy when you can just be angry

rant and rave about how you were wronged

until pages are drowned in rivers of ink

listing all the actions that bruised your dermis.

What's worse is the page stares back at you,

void of words trying to rationalize an ending;

that pain breaks the skin and lingers in your bones

an added weight you carry with you until the grave.

Tell Me Why

Take a census of every vibrating soul

and it could be found that there are two:

those whose gleam in support of others

or those who take a hammer to other hearts

to protect their precious, internalized pride;

fragile enough to crumble when the compass

points success in anyone else's direction.

I used to pray at night for the former

only for you to turn into the latter.

You're Not Sorry

"Can we talk? I'm sorry I hid that from you. Call me back."

"Where are you? I can explain everything. Give me a call back"

"Hey it's me . . . again. Please just hear me out. I can explain. Please pick up. I am so sorry."

"I don't know if you aren't getting these messages or you're just avoiding me but I really need to talk to you. I know it's confusing but please . . . please pick up."

"I know I've said it a hundred times but I'm sorry and I promise it won't happen again. I know I've hurt you in the past but you have to believe me. It's different this time. Alright, bye."

"I saw all your stuff is gone. I can't tell you how sorry I am. This has gotten out of hand. Come back, come back and I will make it up to you."

"I'm sorry. I'm sorry. I'm sorry . . ."

The number you have dialed has been disconnected.

The Way I Loved You

Some loves wrap their arms around you,

put your mind at ease with sweet nothings,

kiss away every fear manifested in your eyes,

bundle you in blissful sheets of sensibility.

Others put you on a tightrope and watch you

balance a fine line between reason and mania.

Every cell of your body filled with adrenaline

and enough love to tilt the scales to insanity.

I've only ever been a trapeze artist

because who the fuck wants easy?

Forever and Always

Words like forever and always

become absolutely meaningless

when you let silence take the place

of your voice on the other end,

signaling I shouldn't ask for a response

because the loud void of words

is one.

<u>The Best Day</u>

When I was young, I didn't understand the storms you faced.
As the tempests that raged outside threatened to shatter every
window; you remained firm, unwavering, sheltering us even
when the bones of your structure feared the potential of
collapse. You hid the stress effortlessly under a haze of warm
bliss wafting through the halls. Completely selfless, ensuring
that this was more than just a house, but a home. I never knew
what days the rain beat against you like a drum because you
made sure that every day, no matter what you were facing, was
the best day for me.

Change

People build walls not for protection, but for containment;

to preserve the delicate balance of what is safely familiar

from that which shakes the ground with the new.

We honor those who can scale such monstrous structures,

bestowing notoriety and praise as if they are Achilles.

But why climb and settle for an edge that's closer to the sun,

to bask in the mundane glory of a hero's welcome.

The demolition of every stone would reveal the stars

with your glimmering constellation among the worthy,

solidifying a seat at the table of the gods.

Jump Then Fall

A breathy Jack Frost morning

warmed by a nectar laugh.

Each sleep drenched syllable

pulls me higher and higher

until I remain suspended there

held by the touch and go

until your gravity takes hold

and pulls me into a free fall.

Untouchable

The only place we share

is the landscape of my dreams

with cursive woven stars

forming my favorite name,

shining as brightly

as the soul radiating off

your god-kissed skin.

I would stay there forever

if it meant having you

close enough to touch.

Come In With The Rain

Investment, I believe is what you called it.

Pouring endless hours you can't get a refund on, into us.

Every dime of free time and every dollar of space

went directly into molding a life together.

But you can't create a masterpiece

with only half of the tools,

half of the manpower,

half of the equation giving a shit.

You called it an investment when you decided to try

and called it betrayal when I stopped.

Superstar

The burn of stadium lights
creating a newborn flush;

rush of crowds at the airport
aiming for a single glimpse;

hopping between time zones
losing all sense of time and home;

another ungrateful, stiff hotel bed
in the evaporated memory of a city;

fuzzy silhouettes in the front row
singing your soul back to you;

a single girl you'll glance at
never knowing her heart is yours.

The Other Side of the Door

The words topple out drunk on anger.

Get in the car.

Leave.

Never come back.

It's not enough.

It's over.

In that moment, every syllable overflows

with freshly squeezed unsweetened pain.

Hours pass and the silence sets in

and each phrase sobers up in remorse.

Get in the car.

Don't ever leave.

Come back.

It's always been enough.

It's never over.

Today Was A Fairytale

With a single glance from your eyes,

the world around us presses pause.

Swirls of golden fairy dust fill the air

in a shower of ethereal bliss.

The hem of your dark grey armor

clings to the salt of your skin

as the west wind lightly breathes,

twirling my dress into a music box.

In the twilight painted air,

extend to me your calloused hand

and let the story write itself.

You All Over Me

God, you're everywhere.

In the stain on my dress from our dinner by the shore,

the painting in my living room you carried in for me,

the coffee maker that always burnt your morning cup,

the memories that tuck me into bed at night when I can't sleep

the outline of dust where our picture once stood on my desk,

even the calendar showing me a day in June I know too well.

I've scrubbed and scrubbed at your touch

and took all planes and trains away from here

but every time I look in the mirror

I am still covered in you.

Mr. Perfectly Fine

It's sad really

disappointing even

how easy I was to forget

almost like you didn't

look in my eyes every night

and tell me the words

you knew would wrap

me around your cool finger.

It's sad really

disappointing even

how for someone who claims

to be so different from everyone

in sheer desperation to be unique,

acting like they own the world,

ends up just like every other boy

whose name I'll forget one day.

We Were Happy

Through stacks and stacks
of shaken statuesque stills
I lose sense of current reality,
wishing only to drown
in welcome antecedence.
Pull me into each moment,
a time free of guilt and
3 a.m. fights and
cordial niceties and
the endless suffocating
that sometimes things don't work out.
To a time where the only things I knew
was your laugh lighting up midnight,
fantasies of your ring on my finger,
and dreamland elation that only comes
in your tender youth.

That's When

Falling asleep next to cold indentations

filled only with the words

your footsteps left lingering in the doorway.

I need some time away to think.

Part of me was ready to pass on

in those somber hours thick with silence

pining for you to raise a white flag.

In a morning blessed by Demeter,

my ears perk to tires in the driveway

and your slamming driver door calling out.

I'll always come back.

Seeing you walk up to my door again

my eyes in California summer sky clarity

I will never want anyone else.

<u>Don't You</u>

amicable

cordial

decorous

civilized

honest

friends

All things that will never apply to us

and will never replace the love

you buried by holding her hand.

Bye Bye Baby

I wanted my heart in your hands

beating firm against warm palms.

I wanted your laugh grazing my neck

as we basked in the sun's glory.

I wanted your spirit to pull me

into cozy, unmarked corners claimed for us.

I wanted your aging skin against mine

watching the miracles we created.

In the end, all I got was your sympathy

singing to me in the solemn key

of your door closing in my face.

SPEAK NOW

"What you say might be too much for some people.
Maybe it will come out all wrong and you'll stutter
and you'll walk away embarrassed, wincing as you
play it all back in your head. But I think the words
you stop yourself from saying are the ones that will
haunt you the longest.

Mine

A list of names we call each other:

In the daytime, to the sound of passing cars
you call me sweetheart.
At night, with your hands tangled in my hair
I call you baby.
In the morning, with light seeping through the blinds
you call me love.
In the middle of the fight, out of senseless frustration,
I call you asshole.
In the midst of walking out, you plead
calling me the greatest thing to happen to you.
When I walk back through the door, you hold me tightly
calling me the only name that could reassure me to stay.

Sparks Fly

Tousled, glimmering chestnut curls.
Emerald globes filled with dreams.
Crescent moon of glowing enamel.
Blooming poppy cheeks in Spring.
Strawberry smirk with my name on it.

A treat for my eyes
like the Fourth of July.

Back to December

Thick, heavy, humid summer
spills over rolled down windows,
sight blinded by the glow of your skin
brushed golden from seasonal heat.

Crisp fall breeze
pull leaves from their resting place
a scene of blended burnt reds and yellows
kiss eyes with lovestruck clarity.

Puffs of warm breath
escape your chapped, quivering lips
visions of happiness sliced in half
daggered by words floating in the frigid air.

Pollen saturated spring
new life swirling around and around
but thoughts remain with three months ago
seen for the first time in 20/20.

Speak Now

You and I have always known it,
the simple truth that soulmates exist;
I am yours and you are mine.
Against endless space and time
we always find our way back to
one another
regardless of the circumstance.
Even now, as you hold her hands
about to swear to a lifetime together
I know it vibrates within you,
that undeniable pull towards me.
Let it take over, look in my direction
towards the future you've always deserved.

<u>Dear John</u>

You looked at life as a chessboard
every person serving a purpose,
a piece in the greater game
hopeful of what the prize entailed.
Your words led me to believe
I sat as the most powerful of all,
the agile and overpowering queen.
I should have believed the others
when they told me I was nothing more
than just a pawn, a soldier for your disposal.

Mean

Someday I'll outgrow you
and your slippery little words
aimed to destroy the confidence
I built with my own two hands.
I'll bask among the stars and the rich
and you'll be where you've always been,
alone with nothing but your opinions
to hold you while you sleep at night.

The Story of Us

You used to call me your Juliet
your other half
your star-crossed lover
your sleepless nights
your reason for being.
The ultimate comparison
of sempiternal love.
It should have occurred to me
that you were calling me
Shakespeare's greatest tragedy.

<u>Never Grow Up</u>

Wish I could run away to Neverland
live with Peter for the rest of my days;
preserve my innocence in glass,
never feel the sting of letting go
of all my simple adolescent joys
I'll take for granted in the moment
yet look back on with utter fondness.
Craving the simplistic euphoria
of knowing nothing at all
and yet everything at the same time.

<u>Enchanted</u>

84 days.
According to science, that's how long it takes.
Eighty-four whole days to fall in love.
You spend them learning each other,
feeling out where trauma begins and ends,
what scars can be seen by the eye
and which ones exist below the surface,
where the heart naturally guides you both
praying it's the same destination in the end.

Then we must be deviations,
anomalies,
outliers,
aberrations.
In flickering seconds, across a crowded room
with the meeting of playful, wandering eyes
I was awestruck, dumbfounded, and above all, yours.

Better Than Revenge

I played the role of a saint
every
goddamn
day
for
you.
Cared and tended to every
whim you so requested.
Purged myself of all I was
to be someone you loved.
Had I known you would leave
for a sinner of notoriety
I would have made a deal
with the king of Hell himself
just to have you in the end.

<u>Innocent</u>

Hide in rocket ships made of cardboard boxes,
trade in these backyard suburban dreams
for unblemished ones of greatness.
Crawl into a simple twin-sized bed
an ocean of green cotton spun waves
let the mind float to visions of screaming crowds.
Carry the lunchbox home with sweating palms
still containing the frowning sandwich crust
that tastes as good as Michelin caviar.

How tragically sad to leave such purity behind
and replace it with the opinions that turn heads
in hopes the spotlight never dims on a childlike smile.

Haunted

I try to run but, again, there you are,
sitting at the usual table in the corner
with that all too familiar Cheshire smirk
as another tries their best to set ablaze
the fire that once raged in my irises.
Your stare leaves cigarette burns
on the soft skin at the back of my neck.
It takes everything in me not to look,
not to turn and run into familiar arms
but that would require your physical body
instead of the phantom of someone I knew
more intimately than the veins in my flesh.

Last Kiss

Dancing in the star-drenched night
to calming silent music;
your thumb driving in circles
at the base of my palm;
hands digging graves in your pockets
as you sashayed to me;
my words drunkenly crashing
against your rude lips.

All the minuscule quirks
that made me want to be
      yours
until my lungs give out.

<u>Long Live</u>

It feels like yesterday:
the angst looming in the air,
glacially peeling the viscous paint
from the crack adorned walls
as the sound of mascara tears
wafts in between each locker,
feeding these halls with nectar
that only ripens in soulful youth.

This is where it happened,
where we stood for a moment
valiant knights, shoulder to shoulder,
high on the desire to be different
immortalized in graduation caps.
For mere seconds, we stood united
coming as many, from lost corners,
and leaving as one.

<u>Ours</u>

Shifting disapproving eyes
with freshly stained lips
whisper slippery verdicts
of how your hand in mine
would make God weep
tears of pity for our souls;
yet still we carry on
rolling the dice of fate
believing in only the luck
we made for ourselves.

If This Was A Movie

Before I knew your name, I would go to the movies
and watch films with formulaic titles tell me of love.
Without fail, affection would blossom in a matter of seconds
shelving any disdain or misplaced pride with the past.
Unsavory circumstance would divide the world into two, both
parties longing for a touch of reassurance from the universe or
each other that everything would heal. By the end, before the
credits flashed, they return home, fate neatly wrapping them
into a package of a happy ending.

After I knew each syllable of your name, I would sit by the
door waiting for the crunch of your tires pulling up the
driveway, for my name at the end of "I'm sorry too" to melt
off your lips, the opening chord of a hopeful love song to play
in the background as you hold me closer than before, gifting a
screenwriter's ending.
Roll credits.

Superman

You made it your business
to go around saving others
protecting their livelihood
conserving a peace of mind
replacing hope with fear.

You do that for everyone,
but you couldn't save me
from breaking my own heart
with the cold uncertainty
of you coming back to me.

RED

"My experiences in love have taught me difficult lessons, especially my experiences with crazy love. The red relationships. The ones that went from zero to a hundred miles per hour and then hit a wall and exploded. And it was awful. And ridiculous. And desperate. And thrilling. And when the dust settled, it was something I'd never take back."

State of Grace

Surrounded in stark cotton
with your hands weaving in my hair
I ask for forgiveness of my past:
for permitting violence on hearts
until they dripped in warm crimson
as tears fled jealous fogged eyes -
loving in blended hues of mistrust.

Kiss away my sins.
Lead me to the clouds.
Bring me grace.

Red

I don't know if I'll ever move on.
All it takes is for my eyes to close,
and the highlight reel starts.

Loving stares from across crowded rooms,
softer touches in dim bedroom lighting,
echoes of laughter scented with coffee.

I can play it faster and faster,
over and over until the images blur
until I see you in only one color.

Treacherous

At the very end of this,
when you break my heart,
or I take a bat to my own,
I'll know it was worth it
because for a sliver of time
I was okay drowning in you.

I Knew You Were Trouble

I should have known better.
You had me the millisecond you walked in
with that abysmal haughty devil of a grin
plastered to a face that would keep me up
for hours and hours as I chased slumber.
I should have seen the signs.
Every godforsaken word you said hooked me,
a new line in the gospel of my life
authored by the shell of the person I became
and ghost written by your poisonous ego.
I should have run.
Hours turned into day and days into weeks
as the clock mockingly ticked and ticked away
until the hands of time halted in place
as you left me there love drunk out of my mind.

<u>All Too Well</u>

I loved you the most at 3 a.m.,
arms reaching for a premature Christmas mug
humming to the lively rumbling refrigerator.
As the dim light carved out your soft dimples,
the glimmer of your irises stirred the galaxy
causing envy in the stars beaming in the night above.
Your subtle expressions aglow by the appliances
watching us fondly as we waltzed through our life,
out of sync and off beat but smothered in strawberry love.

In that hazy fever dream bliss,
is when I loved you the most.
Even now in a different kitchen
in a different city's skyline
I can see you standing there
almost too clearly for comfort.

22

Come, sit here on this spoke.
Take a seat right next to me.
Feel the wood beneath you
as your legs dangle free.
Watch the sky as we move,
slowly downwards at first
just to come back up and
around and around again.
Witness as we pass scenes
of backyard summer pools,
Halloween trick-or-treating,
kisses at the stroke of midnight,
and spring shopping for prom.
Let each memory fade together
into a golden adolescent haze,
overwhelming all the senses
until you're simultaneously filled
with fresh-faced joie de vivre
and prick of precariousness.
Huff it in more and more
until the wheel reaches a stop.

I guess we're adults now.

I Almost Do

One step forward, that's all it would take.
The ground would turn to still air,
my feet treading against nothing.
Fall and fall until your frigid sea
enveloped me in familiarity.
Filling my lungs with sweet nothings
I used to believe were reserved for me.
Lean into the pending hypothermia
while in the midst of drowning
in someone so addictively cruel.

It's all too tempting from for up here,
the floating ice coaxing me.
Just a few more inches and I'm back
submerged in a place I once called home.
I must be a glutton for punishment
to even think of reliving the greatest pain
anyone has dared endure so young.
The thunderous begging crash of waves
fades further and further until I hear nothing
except my retreating boots, optimistic in the grass.

<u>We Are Never Ever Getting Back Together</u>

You always wanted me to call the shots
conjure up every activity, date, and plan,
everything was always my choice.
But when I made the hardest decision -
picked the one thing you didn't agree with
you held my head under a river of blame
let my lungs fill to the brim with guilt.
The cliffside view was my decision
but it was you who inched us closer to the edge
until we were left in nothing but freefall.

<u>Stay Stay Stay</u>

Each time someone came close
to breaking down my exterior
I would quickly exit stage left
leaving the door hanging open,
inviting them to chase me
and pull me back into a world
we were building together.

Consistently I was allowed
to leave without a goodbye,
fleeing in glow of streetlamps
to the sound of heels on pavement
and my aorta being ground to bits.

And now every damn time
I climb out of the passenger side
of your cardboard and duct tape car
I pause, if only for a moment,
hoping you will call after me.

Stay
       because I want you.
Stay
       because I need you.
Stay
       because I can't breathe without you.

<u>The Last Time</u>

I don't want to hear it anymore.
Every time your lips begin to part
my clamped hands rest on my ears.
Stop trying to tell me "sorry"
or that this will never happen again.

The tone in your voice reads as genuine
but every word that drips from your mouth
lost meaning to me a few hundred times ago.
You spent years conning me out of happiness
so I'll rob you of a chance at forgiveness.

<u>Holy Ground</u>

The closest thing to religion I've ever had
was the way your hands held my face
as the belief in your eyes poured slowly
into my own skeptic powdered ones.
Blessing me with newly found faith
is an idea I would have denied until
the last breath my lungs release
diffuses into vapor above my corpse.
Even now as the other half of the bed
stirs only when touched by the cold air
I still believe in the divine guidance
that led your lips to mine.

<u>Sad Beautiful Tragic</u>

When you meet someone new, I hope you tell her everything
about me.
I hope when you put on the striped, blue collared shirt,
you remember I picked it out.
I hope when you order a pizza, you still get extra mushrooms
because that was my order.
I hope during your first kiss, you check your balance
so you don't stumble like during ours.
I hope that when you tell her you love her for the first time,
you take your hands like you did with mine.
I hope that in every single moment you are with her
the memory of me lingers
because no matter how far you run from the regret, like you do
your demons,
everywhere you turn you will see me.

The Lucky One

Now up for auction we have "achieving your dreams".
Shall we start the bidding at sheer talent?
Sheer talent, do I see sheer talent in the room?
Yes, right there to number 78.
Do I hear leaving behind your old life?
Leaving behind your old life to number 243.
Anyone going higher, anything else higher?
Ah, number 165 with changing your personality.
Changing your personality, anyone, anyone?
Number 13 with giving up all personal freedom.
Going once, going twice.
Sold to the woman in the red lipstick.

Everything Has Changed

With "H" it was the reds:
your slightly washed-out lips;
tulips lining the sidewalk;
flush of freckled cheeks.
With "ell" it was the blues:
pristine cotton ball sky;
stormy deep-set eyes;
the used, decrepit car you own.
With "o" it was the yellows:
beating mid-afternoon sunlight;
bees kissing the blooming flowers;
the faded glow of the stoplight.
Combine them together,
let me see in every color
and hear the catalytic word
that changes my world forever.

Starlight

Gentle moonlit eyes
to match a soft curled smirk
and ink-stained fingertips
that graze the small of my back.
The keys and bass enter our feet
injecting an addictive tempo
that leaves us shouting for more
as the band calls for the last song.
One final saxophone loaded hurrah
consumes my blood until I'm intoxicated
on 40s jazz and impossible dreams
fed to me by the stars in your eyes.

Begin Again

I don't remember when I stopped crying,
but I imagine it was somewhere
between the rest stop on I-5
when the moving van popped a flat
and picking out a royal blue couch
because I knew you would hate it.

I don't remember when I stopped writing,
but I imagine it was because you lingered
in all of my clothes from the grey t-shirt
I bought at the fair when you spilled on me
to the gold-plated set of moissanite earrings
you gave me as a sign of misplaced faithfulness.

I don't remember when I forgot your name,
but I imagine it was on a Wednesday
watching the sunset over my chosen city
knowing I could dream in silky peace
as my pain dissolved in a glass of memories
I poured out with the dishes in the sink.

The Moment I Knew

We brought out the fine china,
gracious, delicately laid porcelain,
a sight this house rarely sees.
Overflowing glasses clink in glee
matching the pitch of laughter
that floats from every lively corner.
One setting remains untouched,
the wintry seat saved for you
stares me down across the table.
In a room teeming with delight,
my gaze can only find rest
at an apologetic upholstered chair.
These guests could break every plate,
throw every glass to the scuffed floor
and I would still be the most shattered.

<u>Come Back Be Here</u>

It's all happening too fast
for me to process these feelings.

We're just way too busy
for us to ever make this work.

There's too little time left
for us to savor these moments.

There's too much time left
for me to ponder running after you.

It's too much space
for me to fall in love graciously.

<u>Girl At Home</u>

Peel your eyes off of me,
avert them from my back
and my shirt and my hair.
Stop asking for my sign
or the 10 digits that are mine
when you know hers by heart.
There you go, spending your dignity
as fast as you call the bartender
to pour me another drink on you.
Call your miserable self an Uber,
go home to a soul that deserves better,
pray she can't smell your desperation.

I'll see you in 1989.

ACKNOWLEDGEMENTS

To Kurtie: you are the first person I send every poem to. I cannot thank you enough for encouraging me even when I had very little to be encouraged about; you're the best friend, editor, and fellow writer I could ask for.

To Hannah: thank you for helping me look at each song, edit this book, and supporting me through every step of this journey. Without you, I would be lost in a sea of pretty metaphors and smirking commas.

To Marta: thank you for picking up the phone on December 16th when I first came up with the idea for this book. If it weren't for you I don't know if this book would have seen the light of day.

To Sabrina and Jenelle: your commentary never ceases to bring a smile to my face. The two of you will always hold a special place in my heart and serve as an inspiration for this book.

To anyone who read this collection: from the bottom of my heart, thank you.

FROM THE AUTHOR

Well, hello there. It's wonderful to meet you, I'm Rachel.
I've spent most of my young life writing poems in
journals and on the notes app of my phone while in
crowded places. I never expected to write a book, but alas
here we are. While going through quarantine, I found
myself relating to music again, specifically Taylor Swift's.
With the release of her album folklore, I began writing
sets of poems that were based on songs from the album.
Before long, I had a collection spanning the first four
albums of her discography, resulting in this book. I am
incredibly proud of this body of work and am grateful
that I get to share it with you.
You can find me in the beautiful state of California most
likely drinking mugs tea, dreaming about winter, at your
local record store, or wandering aimlessly around Target.
Thank you so much for reading.

Printed in Great Britain
by Amazon

18084390R00051